D1560599

Don't Juggle Bees!

And other useless advice for silly children

by
Gerald
Hawksley

DO say "please",
if you'd like some cheese.

DON'T attempt to
juggle bees.

DO remember where
you keep your toes.

DON'T balance an elephant
on your nose.

DO shut your eyes
before you go to sleep.

DON'T trust a wolf
dressed as a sheep.

DO keep your
hair on your head.

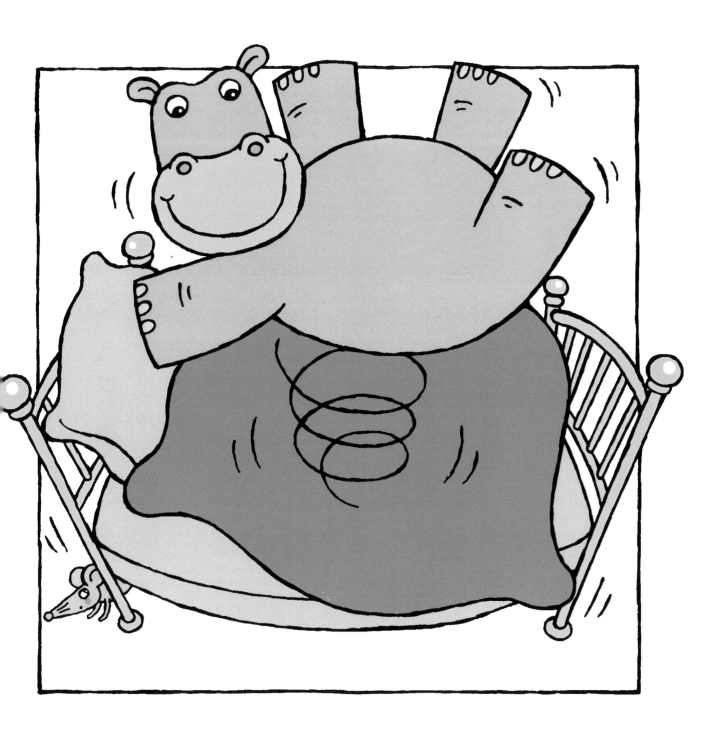

DON'T let a hippo
bounce on your bed.

DO be happy
when you smile.

DON'T share your bath
with a crocodile.

DO start the day
the right way up.

DON'T go to sea
in a coffee cup.

DO wish upon a star.

DON'T let a monkey
drive your car.

DO laugh if you are
ticklish.

DON'T leave your pockets
full of fish.

DO keep your bow tie
straight.

DON'T forget to shut
the gate.

DO sit down on the chair.

DON'T keep mice
in your hair.

DO eat bananas
when you can.

DON'T brush your teeth
with a frying pan.

DO have another
slice of pie.

DON'T swallow a spider
to catch a fly.

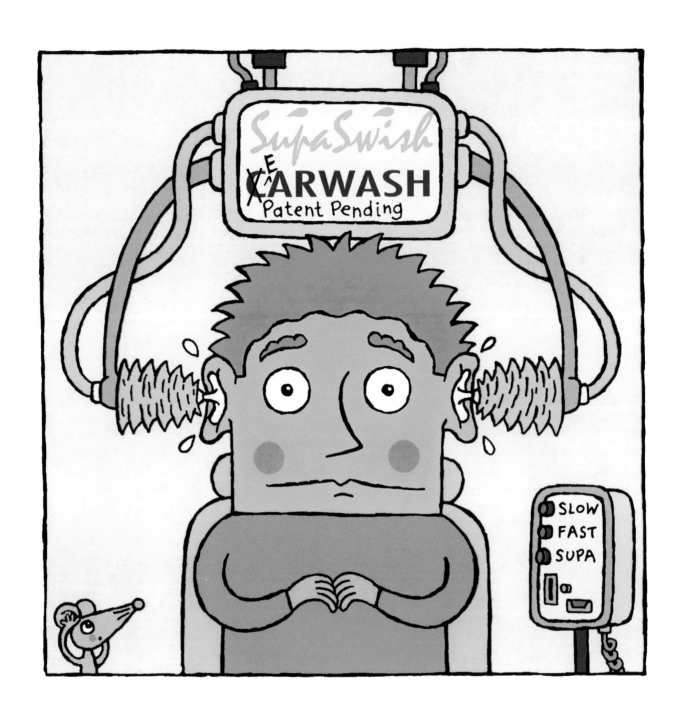

DO keep your ears
nice and clean.

DON'T sow seeds
with a sewing machine.

DO keep your buttons
shiny and bright.

DON'T get lost in the
woods at night.

DO be a faithful,
trusty friend.

And **DO** read this book
right to -

17074701R00018

Made in the USA
Lexington, KY
24 August 2012